Cavalcade Retrospect

Official British Rail Eastern Region Souvenir

Published December 1975 by the Public Relations Dept.,
British Rail, Eastern Region, York

Text and captions set in 10 point Univers Light type,
1 point leaded

Printed by Galava Printing Company Ltd., Nelson

ISBN 0 7003 0031 7

Foreword
by Mr. W.O. Reynolds, O.B.E.,
General Manager, British Rail, Eastern Region

In the foreword to "Cavalcade Reflections", the first book in this series, I expressed the hope that the publication would become a valued souvenir faithfully reflecting the 150th Anniversary Cavalcade and that it would bring much pleasure to countless readers in the years to come.

I am pleased that more than 30,000 friends of the railways have already purchased the book and that the demand for it continues unabated. So many of you have urged the Eastern Region of British Rail to publish more of the photographs taken at the Cavalcade that I am pleased to again lend my support to the production of this companion book to the original.

There have been many requests too for pictures illustrating the intricate and sometimes exacting task which the Region undertook in addition to its normal passenger and freight business, of moving steam engines from all parts of Britain to and from the Cavalcade. Accordingly, pictures of some of these have been included to give in the two publications, a record which is as comprehensive as possible.

I hope you will enjoy this companion book as much as you did the first.

Introduction
by William A. Porter

Creators of Fantasia . . . dealers in magic and spells. Thus did we, mere lineside mortals, revere for a euphoric afternoon, the privileged band who, on sunny Sunday 31 August 1975, created for us the greatest steam show on earth.

The greatest . . . and possibly the last. The Grand Steam Cavalcade between Shildon and Heighington is already part of railway history. But the memory will linger on.

It will linger long in the memory of those like engineer Mike Satow whose talents went into the creation of that magnificent replica of "Locomotion No.1".

"Standing on the footplate of 'Locomotion' as we came under Spout Lane Bridge at a sedate four miles an hour was like bursting from a tunnel into a sun-drenched countryside," he said. "With me on that little train were all the people who had done so much to make 'Locomotion' a reality and the whole event possible. The air of expectancy radiating from the hushed crowd dissolved in a moment the anxiety and fatigue of months. The sun was shining and the beat of the exhaust was music."

For railway author and photographer Eric Treacy, Bishop of Wakefield, there was "magic in the air". It was compounded, he explained, of superb weather, the holiday atmosphere of vast crowds determined to enjoy themselves and "the magnificent machines which crept along the line".

"There was almost a self-conscious air of pride about these engines as they passed before the admiring crowds," Bishop Treacy said. "It was for the British Rail drivers their finest hour, and they obviously realised it. Those who saw it knew that they would never see its like again and knew themselves to be present at an event which would take its place in the history of railways. It was a superb piece of organisation for which we must all be grateful to B.R. and the local committee."

For organising mastermind, George Hinchcliffe, General Manager of Flying Scotsman Enterprises, it was "the greatest railway show ever produced".

"The stars, immaculately groomed, lined up off stage and at 14.00 hours moved forward along a platform five miles long and 30 feet wide," he said. "A vast live audience applauded every single act. The stage manager was well pleased."

For owner of No. 4472, the "Flying Scotsman", Bill McAlpine, it was "magnificent, a fantastic show". For leading Japanese television producer Miss Kaoru Kanetaka, trans-Alps solo baloonist and first Japanese woman to make a land crossing of the South Pole, the event was "simply unbelievable".

For retired education officer Arthur Wickstead, trojan of the assembly area at Shildon Works the Cavalcade had entailed a long night of unbroken hard work for the small team of shunters and drivers arranging the 34 locomotives into Cavalcade order. "It was a long

Introduction continued

night of shunting," he said. "Then at noon on Sunday I called the locomotives one by one to steam out from their sidings over the level crossing, out of our 'section' into B.R. control. All 34 moved across in their correct order without a hitch."

For Geoff Brecknell, Works Manager for British Rail Engineering Ltd. at Shildon, standing by the trackside on that Sunday afternoon "brought feelings of enormous relief that three years of preparation had been brought to a spectacularly successful conclusion".

"Four hundred thousand people had come to savour the majesty of the steam engine, first at an exhibition and then, finally, at the great Cavalcade," he added. "Shildon had emerged into the limelight after 150 years of comparative obscurity. The enormous efforts of hundreds of Shildon Works staff were rewarded in the only way that mattered...by public acclamation."

A full-size replica of "Locomotion" had been completed and tried in steam, but the crucial question remained— was it capable of leading the Cavalcade at the required speed, and without running short of water?

Thus it was that on 23 May 1975, the experiment was tried, and the replica steamed successfully on a return trip between Shildon and Heighington.

Many months of planning and hard work went into the Cavalcade and into the preparation of exhibits, particularly those which had been out of use for years in the Museums at Clapham and York. Here, Midland Compound 4-4-0 No. 1000 undergoes a steam trial at the National Railway Museum, York, on 24 June 1975.

Locomotive movements before Cavalcade day brought a variety of locomotive liveries through York unrivalled since pre-Grouping days. No. 841 "Greene King" is shown on 17 July heading north from the Stour Valley Railway.

Deep in "enemy" territory, crack London Midland and Scottish Railway main-line express locomotive No. 6201 "Princess Elizabeth" steams out of York on 28 July.

On 11 August London Midland and Scottish Railway 2-8-0 No. 8233 and British Railways-built, L.M.S.-designed, 2-6-0 No. 43106 passed through York with a short train of restored vehicles.

Also on 11 August Great Western Railway 4-6-0 "Cookham Manor" passed Class 47 diesel No. 47.431 under the majestic sweeping curve of the York Station roof.

"Workhorse of the night"—Saturday 30 August, 11.30 p.m. North Eastern Railway 0-6-0 No. 2392 engaged on the mammoth task of shunting exhibits in Shildon Works yard.

During the small hours of the night Shildon Yard presents an incredible sight. Plumes of steam . . . drifts of smoke . . . haloes around the lighting towers . . . and brief, lurid gleams as firebox doors are opened and shut.

A night of strange stablemates—North Eastern, Great Western and Caledonian locomotives rest in unusual proximity, waiting for the dawn . . .

As the breeze dispersed smoke and steam, the yard fitfully assumed the aura of a cleverly-lit scene on some fantastic model railway.

Agleam-by-night, the serried ranks quietly simmered, building up their strength for the morrow.

The great day dawns, the dull overcast sky made even more gloomy by a pall of steam and smoke, just like the old days.

The sky lightens, and it is clear that a hard and strenuous night's work has paid off. Most of the locomotives taking part have steam up and are marshalled in correct order.

During Sunday morning, the opportunity was taken to replenish coal supplies at a local yard. London & North Eastern Railway 2-6-2 No. 4771 "Green Arrow" was among those "topped up"—and almost missed the Cavalcade in consequence.

"Green Arrow" with tender tips the scales at around 144 tons in working order—which proved too heavy for the long-disused track in the coal yard, and with only a few hours to go, was marooned on the wrong side of a broken rail.

A concentrated period of work by an experienced British Rail permanent way crew soon had the broken section removed and replaced.

Meanwhile, engine crews went through the necessary ritual of "oiling round". London & North Eastern Railway 4-6-2 No. 4498 "Sir Nigel Gresley" is receiving attention.

Time, too, for a final polish as engine crews and volunteers removed the thin film of grime, which had accumulated during a night of smoke and drizzle, from, amongst others, re-built "Merchant Navy" class 4-6-2 No. 35028 "Clan Line".

Even the highly-polished London Midland & Scottish Railway 4-6-0 "Leander"
benefitted from a last-minute buffing-up of the mirror-like finish of its
paintwork.

A quarter of a mile away, Shildon station was the scene of unprecedented activity, as thousands of spectators arrived on the special shuttle-service of diesel units from Darlington.

As zero hour approached, each exhibit moved slowly out over Mason's Arms crossing, to take its place in an unforgettable buffer-to-buffer line-up ready for "the off"

"Follow the Leader"—rightly enjoying pride of place at the head of the Cavalcade, "Locomotion" replica hauling a chaldron wagon and Stockton & Darlington Railway composite coach of 1842.

The diminutive No. 5 was built in 1857 for the Sandy & Potton Railway and after working as a shunter at Crewe and on the Cromford & High Peak line, it was sold to the Wantage Tramway in 1878. Now preserved by the Great Western Society at Didcot.

"Fenchurch"—a London, Brighton & South Coast Railway locomotive of 1872 leads No. 841 "Greene King", No. 35028 "Clan Line" and No. 41241 of the Keighley & Worth Valley Railway past the Grandstand at Shildon.

Despite a building plate reading "Crewe 1873" London & North Western Railway 2-4-0 No. 790 "Hardwicke" was built in 1892. After withdrawal from service in 1932, "Hardwicke", now kept at the National Railway Museum, York, spent 30 years stored in the paint shop at Crewe works before moving to the former Transport Museum at Clapham.

Built only six years later than "Hardwicke" for the rival Great Northern
Railway, 4-4-2 No. 990 "Henry Oakley" is a much more massive machine, but
shares the same late-Victorian elegance.

Former Lancashire & Yorkshire Railway 0-4-0 Saddle Tank No. 51218, built in 1901, is typical of many small shunting locomotives used in docks and factory sidings where space was limited.

A Scottish visitor, 0-4-4 No. 419 of 1907, drew many admiring glances with her beautiful dark blue livery and elaborate tank-side crests. Scottish Railway Preservation Society hope to run this loco on the Devon Valley line between Alloa and Dollar (in central Scotland in spite of the name).

Rail-level view of the mighty "Flying Scotsman", L.N.E.R. No. 4472, of 1923, passing Heighington. During a working life of nearly 40 years, 4472 covered over two million miles in traffic and in 1968, after preservation, still proved capable of running non-stop from King's Cross to Edinburgh.

No. 7752, a Great Western Railway 0-6-0 Pannier Tank of 1930 built in Glasgow, steams slowly through Heighington. After disposal by British Railways, No. 7752 worked for London Transport, and is now preserved at the Birmingham Railway Museum, Tyseley.

Epitomising the streamlined era, the unmistakable shape of London & North Eastern Railway 4-6-2 No 4498 "Sir Nigel Gresley", built in 1937 On 3 July 1938, a locomotive of the same class, No. 4468 "Mallard", achieved the still unbroken world speed record for steam of 126 m.p.h and No. 4498 exceeded 110 m.p.h on a special train in the late 1950's

Steaming away from Shildon, London & North Eastern Railway B1 Class 4-6-0 No. 1306 "Mayflower" whistles to the crowd admiring her bright apple green livery.

To a post-war generation accustomed to seeing heavy freight locomotives painted black all over, the bright blue boiler and red wheels of former Longmoor Military Railway 2-10-0 No. 600 "Gordon", made a pleasantly startling change.

A controversial feature of some preservation society railways is the painting of locomotives in liveries which they never carried in service. However, few people would deny that No. 41241, a 2-6-2 tank locomotive designed by the London Midland & Scottish Railway but built by British Railways in 1949, made a fine sight with the sun gleaming on her bright red Keighley & Worth Valley Railway livery.

Demonstrating that railway preservation is not an exclusively male hobby, British Railways Standard Class 4MT 4-6-0 No. 75029 "The Green Knight" actually belongs to Mrs Avril Shepherd, wife of the well-known railway artist.

"Last of the line"—No. 92220 "Evening Star"—last steam locomotive in the Cavalcade and last steam locomotive built for British Railways. On completion at Swindon Works in 1960, No. 92220, although primarily a freight locomotive, was given the then standard express passenger livery of lined Brunswick green and an appropriate name marking the end of an era.

The high speed train concludes the Cavalcade and passing the Shildon crowds disappears towards Darlington. Not a shiny show-piece, but a highly successful record-breaking prototype which has already clocked up nearly 200,000 miles of gruelling tests and revenue-earning service.

"After the ball was over"—although most of the exhibits dispersed immediately after the Cavalcade many made their journeys home in easy stages. North Eastern Railway 0-6-0 No. 2392 and London & North Eastern Railway 2-6-0 No. 2005 are seen here at Thornaby.

The Cavalcade running order as planned. Changes included the substitution of N.C.B. 0-6-0 Saddle Tank No. 2502/7 for No. 2779, the inclusion of No. 910 hauled by "Flying Scotsman", and the towing of Great Northern Railway No.1 by "Sir Nigel Gresley" instead of by No. 990.

This and the following pages, giving the running times for each exhibit are facsimile copies from the Special Trains Notice issued in connection with the event.

SUNDAY 31 AUGUST

ORDER OF STEAM CAVALCADE

KEY TO EXHIBIT NO.

1	LOCOMOTION - HAULS CHALDRON WAGON, FORCETT COACH.
2	2779
3	44767
4	2238
5	2392
6	2005
7	419
8	246
9	7752
10	7808
11	6960
12	4771
13	1306
14	8233
15	600 - HAULS 'SARAH SIDDONS'
16	4498
17	4472
18	990 - HAULS STIRLING NO.1
19	790
20	1000
21	5690
22	6201
23	5
24	51218
25	32636
26	841
27	35028
28	41241
29	43106
30	75029
31	92220
32	HIGH SPEED TRAIN

SUNDAY 31 AUGUST

DARLINGTON - SHILDON - BISHOP AUCKLAND

DURING THE PERIOD OF THE 'STEAM CAVALCADE' NORMAL BLOCK WORKING WILL BE SUSPENDED OVER CERTAIN SECTIONS OF THE LINE FOR DETAILS OF PERIODS AND ARRANGEMENTS - SEE SEPARATE INSTRUCTIONS ON PAGES 2 TO 5

CAVALCADE EXHIBIT NO.											1	2	3	4	5	6
TRAIN REP. NO.		2N64	5N64	2N64	5N64	5N64	2N64	5N64	1Z01S	5G10						
FORMED OFF ARRIVAL AT							12†59									
Darlington (Plat.4) Ex. Sdgs.	arr.	12†14	..	12†29	..	..	13 05	..	13 14	..	..	..	..	..	..	..
"	dep.	12 20	..	12 35	..	..	13 05	..	13 14	..	..	..	..	..	..	..
North Road (Signal 847) ..	pass	12 23	..	12 38	..	..	13 08	..	13 18	..	..	..	..	..	..	..
North Road (Signal 845) ..	arr.	..	..	..	..	..	..	..	..	..	..	..	..	..	..	..
" ..	dep.	..	..	..	..	..	..	..	..	..	..	..	..	..	..	..
Heighington	arr	..	..	..	..	..	..	..	13Y27	..	..	..	..	..	..	..
"	dep.	12 30	..	12 45	..	..	13 15	..		..	..	..	..	..	..	..
Shildon (Signal 6) ..		..	12†36	..	12†51	13†06	..	13†36		..	..	..	..	..	..	..
(Down Branch)	arr.		12 38		12 53				Y - Heighington Up Platform							
(Down Platform) ..	arr.						13 20									
" ..	dep.	12 35	12 40	12 50	12 55	13 08	13 20	13 38		..	..	..	..	..	..	..
(Single Line)	arr.	12L36		12L51			13L21			..	..	..	..	..	..	..
(Signal 33)	dep.	12L38		12L53			13L23			..	..	..	..	..	..	..
(Up Platform)	arr.	12 40		12 55			13 25			..	..	..	..	..	..	..
"	dep.	12†46		13†01			13†31			..	..	..	..	..	..	..
(Clear of Signal 6)	arr.	12 48		13 03			13 33			..	..	..	..	..	..	..
DOWN Bishop Auckland	arr.		12†46		13†01	13†14		13†44		..	..	..	..	..	..	..
" ..	dep.	Form 12†51 to Bishop Auckland		Forms 13†06 to Bishop Auckland			Forms 13†36 to Bishop Auckland			13†45	..	..	..	..	..	..
Shildon (Up Platform) ..	arr.									13†51	..	..	..	..	..	..
" ..	dep.										..	..	..	..	..	..
(Up Branch) ..	dep.										14 00	14 02	14 04	14 06	14 08	14 10
Heighington	arr.										14 42	14 44	③	③	③	③
"	dep.								13†32				14 49	14 51	14 53	14 55
North Road (Signal 840) ..	pass								13 39				15X16	15X18	15X20	15X22
													GL	GL	GL	GL
Darlington (Signal 852) ..	arr.								S 5Z01 from Heighington	Forms 16†10 to Heighington	Forms 16 05 to Down Branch Shildon	Forms 16 05 to Down Branch Shildon	15 20	15 22	15 24	15 26
" ..	dep.													15 32		
(Up Sidings)	arr.													15 34		
(Signal 854)	arr.															
"	dep.														..	
(Platform 4)	arr														..	
"	dep.														..	
Sidings ..	arr								13†N47						..	
FORMS DEPARTURE AT																

NOTE : N - Up Siding dep. 14†52 to Clifton C.S.

STOCK : 1Z01 Wickham Saloon
5G10 2 Car Refurbished DMU

KEY TO CAVALCADE EXHIBIT NOS.

1.	Locomotion hauls Chaldron Wagon Forcett Coach	4.	2238
2.	2779	5.	2392
3.	44767	6.	2005

PASSENGERS TRAVELLING ON THE SPECIAL SERVICE BETWEEN DARLINGTON AND SHILDON MUST BE IN POSSESSION OF A CONTROL TICKET.

FOR FULL DETAILS SEE COMMERCIAL CIRCULAR NO.32 DATED 7TH AUGUST 1975 - ITEM 345

S U N D A Y 3 1 A U G U S T

DARLINGTON - SHILDON - BISHOP AUCKLAND

DURING THE PERIOD OF THE 'STEAM CAVALCADE' NORMAL BLOCK WORKING WILL BE SUSPENDED OVER CERTAIN SECTIONS OF THE LINE FOR DETAILS OF PERIODS AND ARRANGEMENTS - SEE SEPARATE INSTRUCTIONS ON PAGES 2 to 5

	CAVALCADE EXHIBIT NO.		7	8	9	10	11	12	13	14	15	16	17	18	19	20	21	22
	TRAIN REP. NO.																	
	FORMED OFF ARRIVAL AT																	
DOWN	Darlington (Plat 4) Ex Sdgs	arr.	..	..	..	..	..	..	..	..	..	..	..	..	..	..	..	..
		dep.	..	..	..	..	..	..	..	..	..	..	..	..	..	..	..	..
	North Road (Signal 845)	arr.	..	..	..	..	..	..	..	..	..	..	..	..	..	..	..	..
		dep.	..	..	..	..	..	..	..	..	..	..	..	..	..	..	..	..
	Heighington ..	arr.	..	..	..	..	..	..	..	..	..	..	..	..	..	..	..	..
		dep.	..	..	..	..	..	..	..	..	..	..	..	..	..	..	..	..
	Shildon (Signal 6) ..		..	..	..	..	..	..	..	..	..	..	..	..	..	..	..	..
	(Down Branch)..	arr.	..	..	..	..	..	..	..	..	..	..	..	..	..	..	..	..
	(Down Platform)	arr.	..	..	..	..	..	..	..	..	..	..	..	..	..	..	..	..
		dep.	..	..	..	..	..	..	..	..	..	..	..	..	..	..	..	..
UP	(Single line)..	arr.	..	..	..	..	..	..	..	..	..	..	..	..	..	..	..	..
	(Signal 33) ..	dep.	..	..	..	..	..	..	..	..	..	..	..	..	..	..	..	..
	(Up Platform)..	arr.	..	..	..	..	..	..	..	..	..	..	..	..	..	..	..	..
		dep.	..	..	..	..	..	..	..	..	..	..	..	..	..	..	..	..
	(Clear of Signal 6)	arr.	..	..	..	..	..	..	..	..	..	..	..	..	..	..	..	..
DOWN	Bishop Auckland ..	arr.	..	..	..	..	..	..	..	..	..	..	..	..	..	..	..	..
UP		dep.	..	..	..	..	..	..	..	..	..	..	..	..	..	..	..	..
	Shildon (Up Platform)..	arr.	..	..	..	..	..	..	..	..	..	..	..	..	..	..	..	..
		dep.	..	..	..	..	..	..	..	..	..	..	..	..	..	..	..	..
	(Up Branch) ..	dep.	14 12	14 14	14 16	14 18	14 20	14 22	14 24	14 26	14 28	14 30	14 32	14 34	14 36	14 38	14 40	14 42
	Heighington	arr.	(3)	(3)	(3)	(3)	(3)	(3)	(3)	(3)	(3)	(3)	(3)	(3)	(3)	(3)	(3)	(3)
		dep.	*14 57*	*14 59*	*15 01*	*15 03*	*15 05*	*15 07*	*15 09*	*15 11*	*15 13*	*15 15*	*15 17*	*15 19*	*15 21*	*15 23*	*15 25*	*15 27*
	North Road (Signal 840)	pass	*15x24*	*15x26*	*15x28*	*15x30*	*15x32*	*15x34*	*15x36*	*15x38*	*15x40*	*15x42*	*15x44*	*15x46*	*15x48*	*15x50*	*15x52*	*15x54*
			GL	GL	GL	GL	GL	GL	GL	GL	GL	GL	GL	GL	GL	GL	GL	GL
UP	Darlington (Signal 852)	arr.	15 28	15 30	15 32	15 34	15 36	15 38	15 40	15 42	15 44	15 46	15 48	15 50	15 52	15 54	15 56	15 58
		dep.	..	15 37		..	15 42		..	..	15 52	..	..	..	..	16 02	..	..
	(Up Sidings)	arr.	..	15 39		..	15 44		..	..	15 54	..	..	..	..	16 04	..	..
	(Signal 854)	arr.	..	..	..	..	..	..	..	..	..	..	..	..	..	..	..	..
		dep.	..	..	..	..	..	..	..	..	..	..	..	..	..	..	..	..
	(Platform 4)	arr.	..	..	..	..	..	..	..	..	..	..	..	..	..	..	..	..
		dep.	..	..	..	..	..	..	..	..	..	..	..	..	..	..	..	..
	Sidings ..	arr.	..	..	..	..	..	..	..	..	..	..	..	..	..	..	..	..
	FORMS DEPARTURE AT																	

KEY TO CAVALCADE EXHIBIT NOS.

7. 419
8. 246
9. 7752
10. 7808
11. 6960
12. 4771
13. 1306
14. 8233
15. 600 HAULS SARAH SIDDONS
16. 4498
17. 4472
18. 990 HAULS STIRLING NO.1
19. 790
20. 1000
21. 5690
22. 6201

SUNDAY 31 AUGUST

DARLINGTON - SHILDON - BISHOP AUCKLAND

DURING THE PERIOD OF THE 'STEAM CAVALCADE' NORMAL BLOCK WORKING WILL BE SUSPENDED OVER CERTAIN SECTIONS OF THE LINE FOR DETAILS OF PERIODS AND ARRANGEMENTS - SEE SEPARATE INSTRUCTIONS ON PAGES 2 to 5.

CAVALCADE EXHIBIT NO.			23	24	25	26	27	28	29	30	31	32		1 & 2 cpld	23,24,25 cpld.
TRAIN REP. NO.													1G10	·X·	·X·
FORMED OFF ARRIVAL AT															
Darlington (Plat. 4) Ex Sdgs	..	arr.	..	..	..	..	..	..	..	..	..	..		..	..
		dep.	..	..	..	..	..	..	..	..	..	..		..	..
North Road (Signal 847)	..	pass	..	..	..	..	..	..	..	..	..	..		..	..
North Road (Signal 845) ..	..	arr.	..	..	..	..	..	..	..	..	..	..		..	..
		dep.	..	..	..	..	..	..	..	..	..	..		..	..
Heighington ..	..	arr.	..	..	..	..	..	..	..	..	..	..		..	..
		dep.	..	..	..	..	..	..	..	..	..	..		16 05	16 07
Shildon (Signal 6) ..	..		..	..	..	..	..	..	..	..	..	..		..	..
(Down Branch)	..	arr.	..	..	..	..	..	..	..	..	..	..		16 47	16 49
(Down Platform) ..	..	arr.	..	..	..	..	..	..	..	..	..	..		..	..
		dep.	..	..	..	..	..	..	..	..	..	..		..	..
(Single Line) ..	..	arr.	..	..	..	..	..	..	..	..	..	..		..	..
(Signal 33) ..	..	dep.	..	..	..	..	..	..	..	..	..	..		..	..
(Up Platform) ..	..	arr	..	..	..	..	..	..	..	..	..	..		..	..
		dep.	..	..	..	..	..	..	..	..	..	..		..	..
(Clear of Signal 6) ..	..	arr.	..	..	..	..	..	..	..	..	..	..		..	..
Bishop Auckland ..	..	arr.	..	..	..	..	..	..	..	..	..	..		..	..
		dep.	..	..	..	..	..	..	..	..	..	..		..	..
Shildon (Up Platform) ..		arr.	..	..	..	..	..	..	..	..	..	..		..	..
		dep.	..	..	..	..	..	..	..	..	..	..		16†10	..
(Up Branch) ..	..	dep	..	14 44 ③	14 46 ③	14 48 ③	14 50 ⑥	14 52 ⑥	14 54 ⑥	14 56 ⑥	14 58 ⑥	15 00 ⑥	15 02 ⑥	..	..
Heighington	..	arr.		15 29	15 31	15 33	..	..	..	..	..	..	15 50	16†17	..
		dep.	..	..	..	..	15 38 16X05 GL	15 40 16X07 GL	15 42 16X09 GL	15 44 16X11 GL	15 46 16X13 GL	15 48 16X15 GL	15 52 ML	16 45	..
North Road (Signal 840)	..	pass	..				16 09	16 11	16 13	16 15	16 17	16 19	16 19	16 54	..
Darlington (Signal 852) ..	..	arr.	..	Forms 16 07 to Down Branch Shildon	Forms 16 07 to Down Branch Shildon	Forms 16 07 to Down Branch Shildon	..	..	..	..	..	..	..	..	..
		dep.	..				16 17	..	..	..	..	..	..	..	..
(Up Sidings) ..	..	arr.	..				16 19	..	..	..	..	..	..	..	..
(Signal 854) ..	..	arr.	..				..	..	..	..	..	..	16 23	..	..
		dep.	..				..	..	..	..	..	..	16*35	..	..
(Platform 4) ..	..	arr.	..				..	..	..	..	..	..	16A 37	16Z 58	..
		dep.	..				..	..	..	..	..	..	16 40	17 05	..
Sidings ..	..	arr.	..				..	..	..	..	..	..	..	..	..

NOTES : A - 1S33 13 00 King's Cross - Edinburgh to arrive Darlington 16 44 dep.16 46   ·X· - Formations 1 and 2 coupled -
Z - 1S27 08 00 Plymouth - Edinburgh to be dealt with at Darlington No.1 Platform.   2779 (Leading)
                                                                                                          Forcett Coach

KEY TO CAVALCADE EXHIBIT NOS.

23.	5	25. 32636	27. 35028	29. 43106	31. 92220	
24. 51218		26. 841	28. 41241	30. 75029	32. HIGH SPEED TRAIN	

Chaldron Wagon
Locomotion

23, 24 & 25 Coupled
32636 (Leading)
51218
5

(column 32 vertical note: To Teesside Airport / 1G11 Heighington to York.)
(column 32: 8)

Acknowledgements

All photographs published in this book are by Ronald Fletcher, Chief Photographer, British Transport Films, York; Ronald J. Hodsdon, Assistant Chief Photographer, British Transport Films, York; Robert W. Anderson, Photographer, British Transport Films, York and J. Stephen Fountain, Photographer, British Transport Films, York.

Captions by Stuart L. Rankin, Public Relations Department, British Rail, Eastern Region, York.

Production and Design by Ronald H. Deaton, Public Relations Department, British Rail, Eastern Region, York.

Issued under the auspices of C. W. F. Cook, Public Relations Officer, British Rail, Eastern Region, York.

"Cavalcade Reflections"

If you have not yet got your copy of the first book in this series, "Cavalcade Reflections", a supply is still available at 65p per copy including postage and packing (UK only) from: Public Relations Officer, British Rail-Eastern Region H.Q., West Offices, York YO1 1HT.

Bonus Offer

And for £1 including postage and packing (UK only), you can secure, from the same address your own copy of the full 30-page Special Trains Notice which governed all movements at the Cavalcade. But there's only a very limited supply. First come first served.